I0151480

APORIAC

poems by

Shey Marque

Finishing Line Press
Georgetown, Kentucky

APORIAC

ACKNOWLEDGMENTS

Some of the poems in this collection have been published previously:

'Nude Descending a Staircase' appears in *Cuttlefish 2015*, and *Award Winning Australian Writing 2015*
'Harlequin Street' appears in *Award Winning Australian Writing 2014*
'a day breaks in two rocks' appears in *Westerly 2014*
'Recess in a River Town School' appears in *Regime 3* (first published as 'Lessons from the Sixth Grade')
'Linger' appears in *Australian Love Poems 2013*
'Nude Descending a Staircase' awarded 1st place: *The Karen W Treanor Poetry Prize 2014*
'Sometimes behind the Wallpaper' awarded 2nd place: *The Kathleen Julia Bates Memorial Poetry Competition 2014*
'Harlequin Street' awarded 1st place: *The Karen W Treanor Poetry Prize 2013*

'I wish to thank the many poets and friends at The Katharine Susannah Prichard Writers' Centre for their ongoing critical support and feedback.'

Publisher: Leah Maines
Editor: Christen Kincaid
Cover Art: Linarie, 'Flows of Doubt' by Linarie Art, www.linarie-art.tumblr.com
Author Photo: Shey Marque
Cover Design: Elizabeth Maines

Printed in the USA on acid-free paper.
Order online: www.finishinglinepress.com
            also available on amazon.com

Author inquiries and mail orders:
Finishing Line Press
P. O. Box 1626
Georgetown, Kentucky 40324
U. S. A.

Table of Contents

Individual poems in this book are dedicated to:

You Over There for Rayma Hagan
Notes on a Bulgarian Music Teacher and Only the Music for
        Radko Bogoyev
Harlequin Street for my family
Recess in a River-town School for Tracy Redwood
Linger and Handstand for Katharine Susannah Prichard
The Flower Paddock for Jennette Foley

'*in the park, rusted songs of swings
just vacated, memories
of play and flight*'

— Kevin Gillam, '*the purpling*'

You Over There

Just tell me what you did today
if only to keep a tiny piece of you in my day
and a bit of me in yours. Ten years of distance
crammed into this email, two sentences
pretend you haven't much to tell. You used to say
our paths ran in parallel. My life could be yours
in as much as yours could be mine.
A neighbour once mistook your knees
for my knees, said that meant we were sisters
or maybe cousins. I never could recognise
the curve of my own profile, the shape of my laugh,
the vocabulary of my walk. Tell me what you see
when you think of me, if ever you do,
if you can still remember how
to help remind me who I am on the outside,
what the back of my hair really looks like.

Another Wasted Day

Killing time with cheap red wine
some bottle incapable of aging
first light I woke, nose bleeding
the bittersweet brightened me
white as meringue, pink like chilli lipstick
the dry eye of morning is upon me.

Untold years have hurtled to the wire.
If there were prints, I never saw them
no tracks pressed into the earth.
They have washed everything white.
In the late morning sun I watch
myself fading, a dog chasing the shadow.

Friday in the City

Only time gives this breeze its name.
Even the air has lost its way, bent
around corners of buildings, diverted
down back alleys. In such a wind you fly
your freak flag like a home-made kite.

The day passes without direction, no
hint of horizon or which way is north.
At night, south is only a calculation,
its crux invisible beneath white noise
of street lamps, headlights and neon.

You wear the chaos like a middle name
inherited from that eccentric aunt,
feel the pull of thread while it knits a cat-
collecting gene into your DNA. As you walk
by an op shop your swivel eye is drawn

to a red beret and purple scarf. You worry
it won't be long before you start drinking
your first martini before noon, and dance
barefoot without music in the street
that day when words are just another noise.

Notes on a Bulgarian Music Teacher

He speaks inside your bones with his past,
haemorrhage of bruised sea on the beach.

Irises, soft and violet, drift back to the war, he
spindle tall as if a flower in the cupboard.

Milk in the soup bubbles over, he says, *and
the burn will leave a slippery cicatrice on your tongue.*

You lay awake on the night of the lost sleep
gleaning for the lesson in his tone.

Insomnia increases life by one third
so he works amid the immortality of darkness.

Through the telescope he sees tranquillity, a place where
everything is round, sharp edges gone.

Last night I saw him sitting on a hilltop, gazing at Jupiter,
reciting poems of silk and cyanide.

He said he was happy.

Only the Music

I teased him a lot that summer
played flat notes in all the wrong places
tuned my own tongue to mimic his
             Baltic inflections
told him that I thought
        con brio means with cheese
just to see his eyes widen
said how fine it was for him
to have all day to devote to music
now he was retired.

By day I worked in haematology
trading afternoon shifts and penalty rates
for evenings at the cello.

Midnight to dawn shift was the hardest to swap
liver transplants had only just begun
all night in theatre they bled and bled
I matched type with type A or B
packed blood in shuttle canisters
sent them into orbit through the hospital arteries.

During the lull at three in the morning
I slumped in the staff room and drank
coffee to keep me awake through hump hour
thought about cello practice and this
regular excuse for not doing any
to be expressed with downcast eyes
ten thumbs and a sigh
the next day.
He half listened to my unimproved piece
        Vivaldi's second sonata in F major
while he spoke of a past career
student at the conservatorium by day
cosmic physicist by night.

I stopped playing to ask when he slept
half hour here
      twenty minutes there
not many about in the small hours.
You and I, he said
we need not be so different.

Watching the Corpse Flower

In the aftermath of lightning surge and hail, you
      see a pine tree encrusted, trunk fractured,
greenstick exposed, like flesh retracted from thigh bone.
      A riven vessel brings palliate glue. You watch how
amber blisters are born, adorn the scars with bling.

Trailing a rage, she crept onto me like that, her welter
      all pearl and lacquer, all talc of soft ash, all
flutter and puff of white dove. I would take her salve
      without passing comment. My inner voice
I knew would be fine with it. After a deluge, you

imagine on limestone hills, a corpse flower, and you wait
      despite the miasma of rotting fish, of ripened
limburger cheese, a tramp's socks. You wait anyway
      just to witness it bloom once a year because it will
be gone again before the day's out.

Siesta in Porto

It was a long walk to the beach
from our room in the city that slept
and kept melancholia as a pastime
we drifted through the afternoon

houses we thought abandoned
their broken windows, peeling paint
the squeak of our cross-trainers
over stone the only sound

but for the old man, cigarette stub
held in the corner of his mouth
leaning on a door post, the load of it all
on his face, his slumped shoulder

a few stray dogs straggled by
heads hung low in empathy or habit
pilgrims en route to the sacred corner
a meeting of mutts inglorious

the skinny one rested on my shoes awhile
as I followed the line of his eye downcast
our chatter upbeat and awkward
anxious to avoid the contagion of sorrow

Angel on a Bicycle

after 'Carnival, Czechoslovakia, 1968' by Josef Koudelka

Wings of cotton at rest, bell untouched, he is pedalling
an ordinary life, keeping pace alongside gypsy horses
marking time with hooves over cobble stone. Exposed

against a background quotidian, boy in white robe plays
silent as a pantomime in which purity is the cameo star
cast as a metaphor for exile. Even from this distance

the rumble of tanks can be felt through the main streets
of Prague. Old woman, hand on hip, watches hope and futility
share the stage as the two old friends become reacquainted.

Alice before Wonderland

after 'Alice Liddell as The Beggar-Maid', 1858, Lewis Carroll

White dress ripped from one shoulder by hands
unmarked of earth, her left breast a new bud,

chichi shedding modesty under a cloud to wallow
ephemeral in sunlight. A sideways glance defies you

to ask, her palm a demitasse outstretched, begging
for grace but her face can't find a pattern for pain.

Hunger is just a name, a figure of pretence
barefoot in crumpled nasturtiums. Picture a waif

standing in a poem by Tennyson, trying on a skin,
Penelophon poised, waiting to catch the eye of a king.

Harlequin Street

I run up the hill after gymnastics. On our front verge my bare legs
pas de chat, flecked with green confetti, catch a shower of grass.

Dad motors over the lawn and laughs. He just misses my batman-
masked brother jump from the garage roof onto the strip of lawn

down the centre of our driveway. Emerging from afternoon shade
my brother springs upright, kneecaps of green. Beside him my sister

fumbling a tape measure and chalk in her hands. Inside, Mum raps
on the lounge room window, wags a finger. Through the flyscreen,

the house smells like grass and cupcakes. I shake off my gym shoes
at the door. Two bags of plaster of Paris lean on the fence, leaking

chalk dust. My siblings' pale faces grin in the kitchen. The cat hisses,
slinks by on her belly. Raw sausage mince thaws on the sink, melts

in my mouth. Fingers plunge into the chest freezer, pull out a fist
of frozen peas which fall like a broken string of pearls. Unwinding,

feet up in front of the television, snifter on the side-table, Dad
yells at the umpire for having only one eye. He doesn't see Bradley.

Outside the boy next door toddles, nappy on his knees, slaps me
and says fuck off. On the lawn his sister Lesley slides into splits,

arms extended, palms splayed, fingers twirl a flourish. I copy her
but get stuck half way. She calls my mum 'aunty'. I shadow her

cartwheels to her back door step. Inside, her mum wipes wine
glasses on her bathrobe. I go to call her mum 'aunty' but the word

hides under my breath. No one is saying hello. Bradley's mum
blows smoke rings at the table, reaches for the aspirin and rum.

The two mothers are trying not to look at each other. The father's flushed face yawns. Down in their henhouse a single rooster crows.

Bradley squeals. His father gives him a Chinese burn and asks if he wants another broken leg. I fall backwards into a bendback.

Later, a knock on our door, Lesley saying her mother won't wake. Dad calls triple zero and runs next door. Mum feeds her spaghetti

and an ice-cream cone piled higher than mine. Outside, a red light from the ambulance flashes while my family watches Roadrunner.

I practise a pirouette and Lesley does the splits. Bradley's mum comes over to collect her early in the morning and I wave goodbye.

As they drive away, their station wagon is stuffed with pillows and running shoes. I turn to see the father's hooded face peering

out of the front room window, red and yellow diamond curtains draped around his body like a clown. Later he is frogmarching

down the drive with two men in suits. On our front lawn, I perform forward flips then stop and fall slowly backwards, hanging there,

I think my face might explode. Next day, Lesley's family still hasn't come home. Again my legs slide over the grass and fail to reach

the full splits. My brother and sister imitate me, giggling. Beside the rubbish bin next door, a stray cat. Empty rum bottles tinkle

as they fall from green bags. Tea leaves from Mum's silver teapot cascade into the rose garden. Mum walks back inside the house.

My family never goes anywhere.

Sometimes Behind the Wallpaper

Down in my grandmother's garden I slip
through the rusty chicken-wire gate
that leads to the old woman's
stone cottage.

Sometimes she catches me trespassing
lures me in with last year's Twisties
held at arm's length until I tell her
my secrets, stay and chat.

She has the features of a toad, squat, rotund,
croaky voice that misses every
second or third word
tongue darts out

over the shedding scales of skin on her lips
as she speaks. Shouts at me over the tv.
Captive inside her lounge room,
I perch

on a sofa that matches the floral curtains. She
sinks into an arm chair that sighs in dust,
her neck puffing in and out
as she breathes.

I ask the whereabouts of her teeth and she tells me
up in Annie's room behind the clock. I wonder
if she could look up there
for my water pistol.

Orange Oil

at the football
my friend and I
fashion a starting line
with sticks fallen from eucalypts

take our marks
bare toes brushing bark
eyes mapping prickle patches
over our running track on the grass

as the siren sounds
we race a hundred metres
all the way back to the picnic rug
to the oily scent of sweat and oranges

her dad in shorts
grass stained whites like his
number thirty one, throws an empty
cool drink bottle at the rubbish bin and misses

he speeds
all the way home
her mum shouting, my friend and I
whispering in the back seat of the purple beetle

Recess in a River-town School

After spelling, the siren will sound and I will
race you to the concrete water fountains fast-
est one there gets the tap with strongest flow

then we head to the canteen crush for mock
cream buns and doughnuts filled with straw-
berry jam. I laugh at your white moustache

on a wooden bench under the veranda, legs
swinging, through plastic packets fingers rust-
ling to find the prized chip, bubble full of semi-

cooked potato. In those remaining minutes, free-
dom before reading and comprehension, we
walk, tap each pole holding up the breezeway

my other arm stretched across your shoulder
yours linked into mine, like those Italian boys
do, and a teacher urges *don't do that girls.*

You whisper *she's afraid we'll turn into lesbians.*

Headhunting

Watching her in the conjoined street
I notice she's looking right at me
unabashed familiarity in her gaze
mixed with a curious indifference
must be golden-haired confusion.

Perhaps she thinks she knows me
I smile a brunette sensibility
she imitates the gesture, smiling
back at exactly the same moment
so I stop and turn toward her.

Absence of even a shadow
vanished by sleight of hand perhaps
transformed into a 'no parking' sign
there again in the shop window
she waits in the last place I saw her.

Linger

On the tilt of my pen   you slide
onto a page etched with inklings of me, inklings of you.

A hybrid being moans in the space between words
gathering speed on its own exhalations.

The air shifts and your skirt parachutes against parchment
sending an echo shuffling towards the open door   and I turn.

I think I hear you in the creaking of floorboards, magpie lyrics,
my own voice, so you can never be gone, not now, not now

You dance atop my feet, light like the child-self,
not quite touching the ground.

Same Formal Cause

With the streetlamp broken I lie curled in a knot,
wait for the timid touch of sleep. In the back
ground I can hear the taunts of youth and you,
you walking in my house in that way you did
so many times before. Its walls bear the chatter,

all our conversations held there, the voice print
bonded to clay. Even after five thousand years
only half will be forgotten or decayed or maybe
this house will be dismantled, all we've said
relocated brick by brick into new lives or maybe

they just crumble to earth always on the cusp
of death or reincarnation. If you held a water glass
to the wall you might hear the rattling of vowels
worked loose with mortar, releasing diphthongs
to the air as they leave through the open window.

In this room we spoke of the mundane things
pavlova and ginger wine, how eating green apples
together with hot tea simulates the sour taste
of vomit or Hershey's. In the ten years since,
my laundry wall has become a fireplace and a brick

barbecue, the occasional door stop. Much of my body
has died, its atoms passed to a lover, or a puppy.
Decades on, even my twin at birth was more like me.
Across my bed, a shadow of things unsaid, or pines.
I don't know exactly what is inside or out.

The Flower Paddock

It must have been a sense of erasure that attracted me
back to that forgotten ground long relieved of our foot prints
I remember you cushioned deep in the grass
      alongside me a jitter of shilly-shally
      smile baked on from squinting too long
      in the sun   a mask of happy
      worn in that way we do as if
      conspired wishing could alter the future
where the flowers took over the earth
      we cut off their heads
      hung garlands around our necks
and pondered the big questions
plucked petals only from dandelions with odd numbers
left alone all those even ones that ended with nots
let loose the skeletons, blew pollen pixies to the unforseen
      as for those tiny new petals too far from maturity to be counted
      only the calyx knows how many it withholds
      how to hide your fate in its pocket

Nude Descending a Staircase

If ever I were to put my hand to clay, take a knife to stone
or dip a mould into molten bronze, it would be to summon
into being this anaglyph from a time when I viewed you as art.

Contour of you frozen in single moments, a series of still frames
under single phase lighting of the stair well. Walk suspended
in mid air. Strobing in the night you are a film star reborn from

a bygone era featuring in an old black and white home movie.
Stepping down through the dark, robe cast in flight behind
your right shoulder, the weight on your back foot, three fingers

pinning the hair from your face. But what features would speak
of sleepiness, complete unawareness of being watched and
preoccupation of events from a nascent dream that leaves behind

a smile which crumples when you catch sight of me standing
there in silence, holding my breath, waiting for you to fall awake.
You demand to know why I lurk so late, scheme to frighten, leave

crumbs in your bed. I touch your hand and lie to you promise
never to do it again, tell you it is me who raids the refrigerator,
makes the mess in the kitchen during the night. Much later

you take those stairs, skin weathered like sandstone in the wind,
somehow rendered precious with time textured to the touch,
a kinetic effigy. Only this time you don't stop humming Bellini's

melody from *La Sonnambula*. Ballerina you just float by in bel canto.
I wish I could recall the song's title however the name eludes me
as many names do. Something in me of you. I wonder aloud if you

feel cold, your skin exposed to the night, but get no response
of the verbal kind. Red scarf hanging on the coat rack, winds
its woollen way around your neck a second before the front door

closes. A street lamp outlines you, turns you into a light painting.
I find I have become Balanchine's poet, hesitant to wake you
into ignominy, yet too afraid not to should you plummet in sleep.

So I shadow you in *pas de deux*, try to catch the rhythm of your feet,
fathom the purpose in those eyes beneath their mask of glass, feel
the weight in your arms as I bring you back as the final act is sung.

Early morning I blink, brush away white salt and pine needles to find
bruises on both shins, my clothes scattered over the wooden steps.
Waves roll in, threaten to erode this sculpture of you in the sand.

Handstand

Long after the tide has cleared those footprints from the beach
        I stand at the edge of a picture, watch your fingers
take root in weathered castings of cuttlefish and shell, dunes
        behind me, laced with wild weeds, your humid salt
on the wind, on whitecaps, on my face, on my tongue. Sinking
        through the emulsion, I stumble back to you, turn
black and white, share your upside down view of the west, let
        loose change fall from my pocket, hear its soft thud
to earth. Fine sands lift across the shadows of clouds, a chain
        bearing your name tumbles from around my neck,
glint of the key to your cottage on the hill. I wink, whisper
        behind my hand, confide in you my discovery
of that secret hiding place among the thorns of Bougainvillea.

Imagine becoming the sea

Sand
speckle dusted
across belly skin

Inch
by inch
mimic a dune

Me
sculpture hatchling
on the shore

Layers
dissolve gradually
palimpsested by sea

The Tweening

Her bones lie damp where they point to the wreck   beckoning
    to the ghosts of sailors   to the fallen   the unwary.
She sifts through skeletons in her cellar beneath the sea   mere
    mementos to keep track of time and travellers past.
She layers seconds into eras and preserves them in brine shakes
    to watch them fall again glitter in her water dome.

The sinklings tell of a lost Atlantis   and the beasts of arcady
    in the end unable to bear the sky.   Once dolphins
filliped within her belly common as herring somersaulting
    and bird men rallying   all wing and feather on
summer days   a headier century   when we still believed
    we could fly.   Now all bound to salt and dust of lime.

A chain of vertebrae   hollow and scoliosed with age   anchors her
    wetlands to the underworld   melds fiction to the real.
Miniature shrimp scamper in her hipbones   shelter in open pockets
    bat wings tickle her sinuses   blind to the notion of loss
mosquito fish coalesce in foreign codes   going over her head
    wild turkeys comb through bulrushes looking for rain.

Reveries pour from her cavernous mouth. Doorda Mia yawns
    where wild dogs sleep. Dreams leak paint   into her lakes
water colours stream into wetlands where she washes   stories
    from brushes on the banks of Pipidinny.   Tweening
inertia of unstill life   transforms a civilisation from antiquity
    to fantasy and fable   a Sun City   with a rock for a king.

The Settling of Wrecks

Folk here are of salt and lime, one eye always drawn to water.
If they look away too long they won't notice traps set by the sea
and Two Rocks beach can be lavish with treachery and strays.

Few symbols to name such a place. Two pillars of limestone.
That there weren't a couple of dogs mating on the beach that day
is fortunate enough. Pointers to the wrecks. It's just the spot

to catch a wave or whiting, herring and blowfish (in my hands,
reverse that order). Seaweed festers upon dog beach. Fumes
from boat and four-wheel drive fuel mist the air at the marina.

Our community is boat shoed and thonged. Neptune still presides
over the town, grocer pushes trolley trains, baker chain smokes
in the sun, the almost homeless from apartments above cast out

prophecies from their balconies. Village street signs will remember
only yachts; America's Cup challengers from two centuries. Dame
Pattie and Gretel retire gracefully alongside Sappho, Valkyrie and

other fast women long since fallen into disrepair. We have cribbed
beaches from the wishing well where a trail of guilders and other
old coins once littered the sea beds. In this museum without walls,

wrecks exhibit on reef and seagrass meadow. We sit on fretted
dune, watch the demise of the sun, lick crusted salt from cuts and
margaritas, swap stories about past marriages and other ruins.

After Moving to the Coast

The shape of us shifted
for all I could tell
we were blue-eyed Selkies
          wailing low and long
salt-strong
colour of the night sea
dark-maned and muscled.

The moon turned a blind eye
that night   we disappeared
below the surface to dance
when we came
                    back up for breath
you licked at the ocean
          as it rolled
                    from my cheek
I couldn't tell if I cried.

How far away they seemed
          those city lights searching
a sky winking.

On the beach
miniature sand crabs
watched on   bug-eyed
waiting to collect
          our   shedding   skins.

a day breaks in two rocks

blue is the shipping beacon, the scythe
in the sky, the exposed roots of yachts, the
squeak of drying, the spinifex skipping. blue
is monday morning. blue is two buoys squat-
ting, the ropes on their necks, the ears on the
sand, the crab holes winking, the large bowel
of beach. blue is monday morning. blue is the
last spit of summer, cray boats in arms, the
muscles clinging beneath, the forgotten gate
propped open, the no-swimming sign. blue is
monday morning. blue is the sanskrit sea, the
echo of a father's voice, two canvas shoes
parked on the jetty, a kiss on the sea bed, the
police light flashing. blue is monday mourning.

The Changing Skin of Drowning

He had too many that last time   he left us
with six live ones
a catch that was thorny sweet

Today the sirens are quiet. Paul doesn't hear them coming
                    for him. Veiled in salt cloud
he and a buddy collect Western Rockies from their pot, its rope
        a scribble   winds a knot of the Gordian kind
around his ankle. Undone   shouting bubbles
snatching fists of water   a knife   falls.

His buddy stops catching crays but returns to the reef
            stares out at the rip current   again and again
lungs catch on a pang he mistakes for empathy
or adage
            because we really aren't fishes
and for five months carries a fisherman's words
            dive today and tomorrow I will dress in black.

Walking down the wooden stairway to the sand   for weeks
people are drawn to posies tied with spear grass   to the handrail
        blue butterflies hover over saltbush.

Sometimes at night   a butterfly of blood red   swells
          inside the buddy's chest grown so
that no manner of coughing can work it loose.
He thinks of invisible things   like Paul
          crocidolite   friable filaments on the wind
snacks on apricot kernels and berries
                    shallow breathes from his mask.

The day he too drowns   in air
neighbours gather on a balcony overlooking the sea   drinking
          drinking in the symmetry   in the doubling habit of fate
I notice the street heavy with wild rosemary
its bloom of bruise
                    colour of storm cloud   relentless sea
                    and the reckless earth of Wittenoom.

Storm on the Swan
from 'Storm on the Swan' by Elise Blumann

I wonder if the trees knew a storm was coming
leaves turned upward to catch the falling rain
or if they purged the river through their veins
then made it rain by way of humble dance.

River blurs a boundary and lets in the sea.
The shifting space of air and water, the new
softness of limits, its sense of self melds
with the earth and the shadows of trees.

Limbs horizontal in the slipstream paddle
naked in the rain. The weather disrobes
rearranges itself, brazen before the artist's eye
then settles into character for the day.

Tilt your head. Inhabit the blur. The sky could
resemble the river, or the river the sky. Either way
this is a rain in which you could tumble-turn,
wear under your skin on a humid day.

I search the space in my head for scud clouds
travel back in time to the town of Lajamanu
where the sky and the river changed places
picture that swarm of spangled perch

as they fall from the sky, their forked tails,
pectoral fins useless to paddle in air.
Somewhere, I thought, there must be a cat
rubbing a pearl shell, performing a rain dance.

Shey Marque lives and writes in the coastal town of Two Rocks, Western Australia, with her husband and two dogs. She holds a PhD in the medical sciences and worked as a hospital haematology scientist in Australia and New Zealand before moving to Dijon in France where she taught English while studying French language.

In 2011 she completed a Master of Arts in writing and worked until 2013 as Coordinator and board member of The Katharine Susannah Prichard Writers Centre in the Perth hills where she remains a member of the poetry community.

Currently, she is Coordinator of Hospital Poets Australia, an initiative founded in 2010 by Anna Soter for The Ohio State University's Medicine and the Arts Program.

An award-winning poet, she has twice won The Karen W Treanor Poetry Prize in addition to various places in other competitions. Her poetry is published in literary journals including *Cordite Poetry Review, Westerly, Award Winning Australian Writing 2014,* and *2015, Australian Love Poems 2013* and others. *Aporiac* is her first chapbook collection.

www.ingramcontent.com/pod-product-compliance
Lightning Source LLC
LaVergne TN
LVHW051611080426
835510LV00020B/3247